Apr. 28, 2010

D0848308

Nature's Secret Habitats Science Projects

ANN BENBOW AND COLIN MABLY

ILLUSTRATIONS BY TOM LABAFF

Enslow Elementary
an imprint of

 Enslow Publishers, Inc.
40 Industrial Road
Box 398
Berkeley Heights, NJ 07922
USA

http://www.enslow.com

Enslow Elementary, an imprint of Enslow Publishers, Inc.

Enslow Elementary® is a registered trademark of Enslow Publishers, Inc.

Library of Congress Cataloging-in-Publication Data

Benbow, Ann.
    Nature's secret habitats science projects / Ann Benbow and Colin Mably.
      p. cm. — (Real life science experiments)
    Includes bibliographical references and index.
    Summary: "Presents several easy-to-do science experiments about habitats, and provides explanations for their outcomes" Provided by publisher.
    ISBN-13: 978-0-7660-3150-0
    ISBN-10: 0-7660-3150-0
    1. Habitat (Ecology)—Experiments—Juvenile literature. 2. Animals—Adaptation—Experiments—Juvenile literature. I. Mably, Colin. II. Title.
    QH541.14.B475 2010
    577.078—dc22
                                                      2009012114

Printed in the United States of America

10 9 8 7 6 5 4 3 2 1

To Our Readers: We have done our best to make sure all Internet Addresses in this book were active and appropriate when we went to press. However, the authors and the publisher have no control over and assume no liability for the material available on those Internet sites or on other Web sites they may link to. Any comments or suggestions can be sent by e-mail to comments@enslow.com or to the address on the back cover.

♻ Enslow Publishers, Inc., is committed to printing our books on recycled paper. The paper in every book contains 10% to 30% post-consumer waste (PCW). The cover board on the outside of each book contains 100% PCW. Our goal is to do our part to help young people and the environment too!

Illustration Credits: Tom LaBaff

Photo Credits: Associated Press, p. 16; Brandon Cole/Visuals Unlimited, Inc., p. 36; Eddy Lee, p. 12; Enslow Publishers, Inc., p. 40; Shutterstock, pp. 20, 24, 28, 32; © 2005 Walter Siegmund, p. 44; E. Widder/HBOI/Visuals Unlimited, Inc., p. 8.

Cover Photo: Shutterstock

Contents

Experiments with a 🎀 symbol feature **Ideas for Your Science Fair.**

Introduction

A habitat is a place where living things, or organisms, live. There are many different kinds of habitats. Some are wet and warm, others are hot and dry, and still others are cold most of the time.

Living things are adapted to their habitats. This means that their shapes, colors, sizes, parts, and food sources fit, or are suited to, their habitats. Organisms that live in the same habitat may depend on each other for food, shelter, and the other things they need to survive.

You can use this book to investigate many things about habitats. You will be asking questions about habitats, doing experiments, making observations, and finding answers about them. By the end, you will know a lot more about habitats than you do now. You will also know more about science!

Science Fair Ideas

The investigations in this book will help you learn how to do experiments. After every investigation, you will find ideas for science fair projects. You may want to try one of these ideas, or you might think of a different project.

This book has a Learn More section. The books and Web sites in this section can help you with science fair projects.

Remember, science is all about asking questions. A science fair gives you the chance to investigate your own questions and record your results. It also lets you share your findings with your fellow scientists.

Safety First!

These are important rules to follow as you experiment.

1   Always have **an adult** nearby when doing experiments.
2   Follow instructions with care, especially safety warnings.
3   Never experiment with electrical outlets.
4   Use safety scissors and have an adult handle any sharp objects.
5   Use only alcohol thermometers, never mercury!
6   Stay in a safe place if making outdoor observations.
7   Treat living things with care. Some may sting or be poisonous!
8   Keep your work area clean and organized.
9   Clean up and put materials away when you are done.
10 Always wash your hands when you are finished.

Experiment 1
What Lives Under Stones and Logs?

What do you think you would find if you turned over a flat stone or log? Write down your ideas and your reasons for them.

Now Let's Find Out!

1 With an adult, go outdoors into an area where there are flat stones or logs. This experiment works best if the stones or logs have been in the same place for six weeks or more.

Things You Will Need

an adult

outdoor area such as a garden, park, or yard

log or large, flat stone

gloves

magnifying glass

notebook and pencil

2 Look at the ground around your stone or log. Is it wet or dry? Is it warm or cool? What plants or animals do you see? Record your observations in your notebook. What kinds of plants or animals do you think might live underneath the stone or log? Talk over your ideas with your adult partner.

6

3 Wearing gloves, your **adult partner** should now gently turn over the stone or log. What is the habitat like underneath? What living things do you see with just your eyes? What do you see with a magnifying glass? How are they the same as the living things that live around (but not under) the stone or log? How are they different? Why do you think they are different?

4 When you are finished making and recording your observations, have the **adult** carefully put the stone or log back into place.

What Lives Under Stones and Logs?

An Explanation

It is dark and usually damp under stones and logs. The living things in this habitat are suited to these conditions. You might have found isopods (pill bugs). The darkness under a stone or log shields them from the light, which helps keep their skin moist. These animals have many short legs, which help them to move in small spaces.

FACT: Animals that live in dark places (like under stones and in the deep ocean) have special adaptations to live there. One deep ocean dweller, the female angler fish, has a "fishing rod" attached to its head that glows in the dark to attract prey!

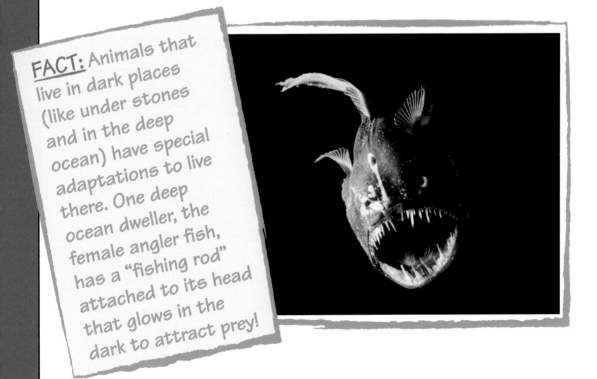

Earthworms, salamanders, and grubs (larvae of beetles) can also sometimes be found under stones and logs.

Ideas for Your Science Fair

- What is the difference in temperature between the ground around a stone, and the ground under the stone?

- Are there more living things under logs in the winter or in the summer?

- How long does it take a living thing to make its home under a stone?

Here is a look at some life under a stone.

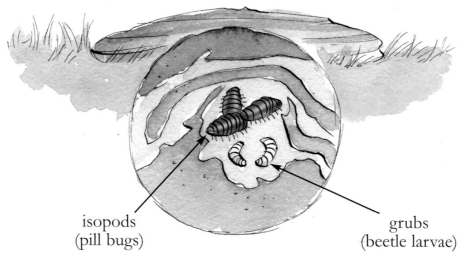

isopods
(pill bugs)

grubs
(beetle larvae)

Experiment 2
What Materials Make Good Birds' Nests?

What birds' nest materials are the most flexible? Write down your ideas and your reasons for them.

Now Let's Find Out!

1 Cut a twig, a piece of broom straw, and pieces of dry and fresh grass all to the same length, about 12.5 cm (5 in).

Things You Will Need

thin, dry twig
broom straw
fresh grass
dry grass
safety scissors
protractor
notebook and pencil

2 On a table, hold a protractor upright in front of you. Now lay one of the test materials alongside the protractor with its center at the midpoint. Use a finger to hold the material down in the center. Then with your other hand, bend the end up until the material snaps.

Hold the protractor with your hand, and the material with your finger.

Push up until it snaps!

3 Measure the angle on the protractor at which the material snapped. (Some may not snap.) Write down the angle in your notebook.

4 The material that snapped at the smallest angle is the least flexible. Line up your nest materials from the most to the least flexible. Which material could birds bend easily to shape their nests? Which material was the least flexible? How do you think a bird could use this material to make its nest strong?

What Materials Make Good Birds' Nests?

An Explanation

Nests come in different shapes and sizes. Birds' nests can be found in trees, vines, shrubs, or even on the ground. Different birds build different nests. Many birds use flexible materials like grasses and vines to make their nests bowl-shaped. Some use less-flexible materials like twigs and straws to give the nests strength. Birds build their nests to

FACT: For many years, people in China have made a rare type of soup out of bird's nests. They use nests made by a bird called a swift. Swifts use their own gummy saliva to build nests on the walls of caves. The nests, which are totally edible, are harvested to make the soup.

be light, strong, warm, and in safe places. This way the nests will hold eggs until they hatch and then protect the young birds as they grow.

Ideas for Your Science Fair

- What materials do birds use to keep their nests warm?

- How do birds get their nests to stay in place after they build them?

- Where do birds get the materials they need to make their nests?

Birds' nest-making materials

dry grass   vines and twigs   sticks and twigs

How Are Fish Adapted to Living in Water?

What features do fish have that suit them to underwater life? Write down your ideas and your reasons for them.

Now Let's Find Out!

1   You can use your own aquarium for this experiment. If you do not have an aquarium, you can use one in a pet store, at a friend's home, or in your school.

2   Carefully observe the fish in their watery habitat. What parts help the fish to swim? Do some fish seem to move more quickly through the water than other fish? Why do you think this is so?

3   What parts do the fish have that help them to breathe

Things You Will Need

aquarium with plants and at least two different types of fish (goldfish and guppy, for example)

notebook and pencil

underwater? Do all of your fish have the same kinds of parts that help them to breathe? Write down your observations.

4 Does one fish seem to blend in with the plants better than the other? Why do you think fish might stay around plants in their habitats? Again, note your observations.

5 When you stay in the water too long, your skin can get all wrinkly. Scientists are not yet sure why this happens. One idea is that water washes away protective oils that are usually on your skin. How are the fish protected from becoming wrinkly in water?

How Are Fish Adapted to Living in Water?

An Explanation

Fish have gills that take oxygen from the water into their bodies. They have a streamlined shape and fins to move through the water easily. Many fish have scales. Scales protect a fish's skin from sharp objects and damage. They also stop a fish's skin from becoming wrinkly. Some fish have colors or

FACT: The Georgia Aquarium in Atlanta is the world's largest aquarium. It also has two of the world's largest fish. The whale sharks at the aquarium can grow to over 12 meters (40 feet) long!

body parts that help them blend in with plants. Blending in helps fish stay safe from predators.

 ## Ideas for Your Science Fair

- How are freshwater and saltwater aquarium fish adapted to their habitats?

- What types of aquarium fish find what types of aquarium plants attractive?

- How do aquarium fish behave when you add a small toy or object to their habitat?

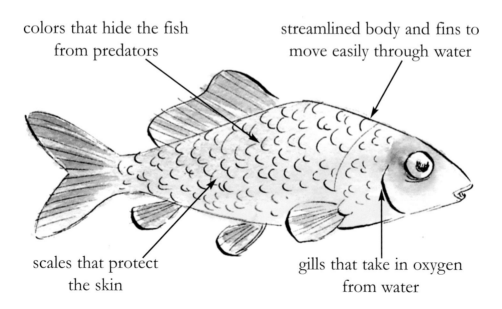

colors that hide the fish from predators

streamlined body and fins to move easily through water

scales that protect the skin

gills that take in oxygen from water

Experiment 4
How Does Color Help Animals in Habitats?

How do you think that an animal's coloring helps it fit into its habitat? Write down your ideas and your reasons for them.

Now Let's Find Out!

1 **With an adult's permission**, go outdoors with your notebook and pencil. You may also find it useful to bring binoculars, if you have them.

2 Pick a quiet place in the area where you can observe birds, squirrels, chipmunks, insects, frogs, or other animals. Find a place in this area to sit quietly, so that the wildlife will not be frightened away.

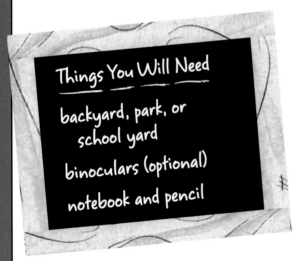

Things You Will Need

backyard, park, or school yard

binoculars (optional)

notebook and pencil

3 First, observe the animals using just your eyes. Then use binoculars if you have them. Are animals in trees,

18

on shrubs, on the ground, or elsewhere? What colors are the plants and soil around the animals?

4 How well do the animals' colors blend in with their habitats? How do you think this blending in helps the animals find food, sneak up on prey, or avoid being eaten by predators? Some animals do not blend in very well. Why do you think this is so?

How Does Color Help Animals in Habitats?

An Explanation

One way in which animals are adapted to their habitats is their color. You may find it hard to spot brown, black, or grey birds against tree bark or to spot green insects on leaves or grass. Blending into the background like this is called

FACT: The chameleon is a lizard that changes the color of its skin to suit its background. Chameleons can do this because they have special cells in their skin with different types of pigments. They also change color to make themselves look better to their mates!

camouflage. Camouflage helps the animals to survive and reproduce because it makes it harder for predators to see them. Some other animals have brightly colored bodies, which scare away predators.

Ideas for Your Science Fair

- How do animals blend into a snowy habitat?
- Why do female birds usually blend in with their habitat better than male birds?
- In what situations can an anole (type of chameleon) turn a color other than green?

Experiment 5

How Do Habitats Change From Spring to Summer?

How do habitats in your area change from one season to the next? Write down your ideas and your reasons for them.

Now Let's Find Out!

1   This investigation will take a few months! Choose an area in your backyard, school yard, or nearby park that has lots of plant and animal life.

2   Start your observations in the early spring and end in early summer. In your notebook, record the date of your first observation and the day's weather conditions (temperature, cloud cover, amount of precipitation, and how windy it is).

Things You Will Need

outdoor area with plant and animal life

thermometer

camera (optional)

notebook and pencil

3   Write down the types of plants

and animals you observe in a certain area. Record the sizes of the plants, and note if they have leaves and flowers. Draw this area or take a picture. Be sure to put the date on your picture or drawing. Continue to make observations and take or draw pictures every two weeks in the same place.

4 After at least three months, look over all your data. How did the habitat you observed change from spring to summer? How did the plants and animals change? Why do you think this happened?

How Do Habitats Change From Spring to Summer?

An Explanation

The living and nonliving things that make up a habitat can change throughout the year. In parts of the United States where the temperature changes a lot from season to season, habitat changes are easy to see. In spring, for example, the weather gets warmer and there is more sunlight. Trees and shrubs start budding. You will also see plant shoots begin

FACT: In the desert, there is very little rainfall. Sometimes many years may go by with wildflowers hardly blooming. But if it rains and the conditions are just right, wildflowers can fill the landscape with a blaze of color.

Plants bloom in a desert.

to come through the soil. Insect eggs hatch and birds fly back from their winter homes.

From spring through summer, young plants and animals grow, which changes the look of the habitat.

 ## Ideas for Your Science Fair

- How does your local habitat change after a big storm?

- How does your local habitat change from fall to winter?

- How does your local habitat change when a new road or development is built?

Spring   Summer

Are Food Chains Different in Dry and Wet Habitats?

Are there differences in how organisms get their food in dry and wet habitats? Write down your ideas and your reasons for them.

Now Let's Find Out!

1 Choose a warm, sunny day to make your first observation. Go outdoors with an adult to a dry area, such as a backyard or a park. Find a quiet spot to sit.

Things You Will Need

an adult

dry, outdoor area with plant and animal life (school yard, park, large garden)

outdoor area near a pond or stream

notebook and pencil

2 Observe the plant life. What animals are eating the plants? What animals are eating other animals, such as birds eating insects or worms? Look at the ground around you. Push aside plants to better see the ground. Record all of your observations including what eats what.

26

3 Now, go with **an adult** to an outdoor area near a pond or a stream. Record the same observations as in step 2.

4 Go back to your observation areas several times over the next two weeks when the weather is nice. Record what you see.

5 In your notebook, draw a diagram showing how the different organisms you observed depended on each other for food. This is a food chain. How are the "dry land" food chains different from the "waterside" food chains? Why do you think this is so?

Are Food Chains Different in Dry and Wet Habitats?

An Explanation

Your "waterside" food chain is made up of organisms that live in or near water, such as fish, frogs, and duckweed. Your "dry land" food chain is made up of organisms that like a drier habitat. Depending on where you live, these could be oak trees, cacti, squirrels, grasshoppers, and robins. Food chains start with plants. Plants make their

FACT: Males and females from the same species can have different roles in food chains. For example, a male mosquito eats nectar, which makes him a plant eater. Many female mosquitoes will also feed on blood, which makes them both plant and animal eaters.

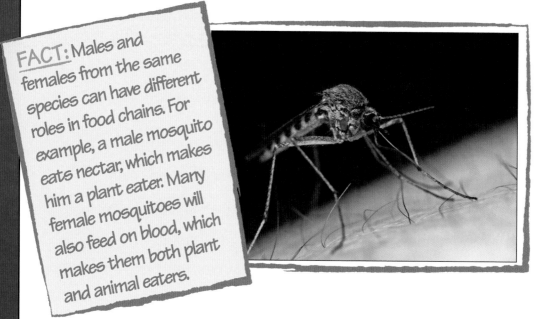

own food from carbon dioxide, water, and the sun's energy. Animals that eat the plants come next in the food chain. Next are animals that eat other animals. At the end of food chains are "decomposers," such as fungi or bacteria. You will not see them actually eating, but they consume dead animals and plants and turn them into nutrients.

 Ideas for Your Science Fair

- What food chains are under rocks?
- What food chains are in soil?
- How are food chains different in the summer and in the winter?

grass
(plant)

grasshopper
(plant eater)

insect-eating bird
(meat eater)

Experiment 7
How Varied Can Two Habitats Be?

Do the habitats in your area have many types of organisms or just a few? Write down your ideas and your reasons for them.

Now Let's Find Out!

1   In warm weather, go to a mostly natural habitat with **an adult**. Explore the area and record how many different types of organisms you see. Take photographs of them if possible. It is not important that you know all of their names. Just be sure that you can tell that one is different from another.

Things You Will Need

an adult

local habitat that is mostly natural (yard, field, park)

local habitat that is mostly built up (area around parking lot, playground, tennis court)

camera (optional)

notebook and pencil

2   In similar weather, go to a habitat that is mostly built up. Would you predict that

there would be more or fewer different types of organisms here? Why do you think this? Repeat observing, counting, and recording for this habitat.

3 Revisit both of these habitats over the next two weeks, making two more observations for each. At the end, add up the different types of organisms in each habitat.

4 Which habitat had the most diversity (different types of organisms)? Why do you think this is so?

How Varied Can Two Habitats Be?

An Explanation

Living things depend on each other for survival. In habitats with many different types of living things, it is more likely that there will be materials for shelter and a good food supply. You probably found more organisms in the natural area than in the built-up area. When areas are covered with concrete or other building materials, natural habitats can

FACT: Some species take over a habitat if they are not stopped. These "invasive species" can keep other organisms from surviving in that habitat. The kudzu vine, which was brought to the U.S. from Japan, spreads so quickly over acres of land that it covers the soil and trees and keeps other plants out!

disappear. The organisms that lived in those habitats either died or moved away.

 ## Ideas for Your Science Fair

- What can people do to attract different types of living things into their gardens?

- What "invasive species" do you have in your area?

- Does your backyard or school yard have more species in the fall or in the spring?

wild area

paved area

Experiment 8
Can Plants Adapt to Different Habitats?

What happens to plants that live in water and plants that live on land when you move them to different habitats? Write down your ideas and your reasons for them.

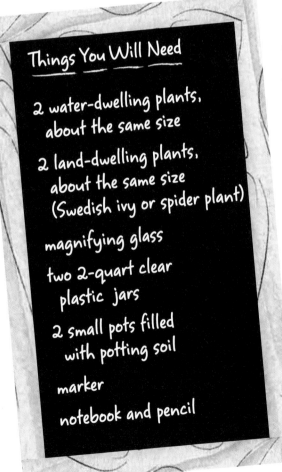

Things You Will Need

2 water-dwelling plants, about the same size

2 land-dwelling plants, about the same size (Swedish ivy or spider plant)

magnifying glass

two 2-quart clear plastic jars

2 small pots filled with potting soil

marker

notebook and pencil

Now Let's Find Out!

1 Look at the leaves of the water-dwelling plant just with your eyes, and then with the magnifier. How is the plant suited to living in water? Are its leaves thin or thick? What kind of roots does it have? Now look at the land-dwelling plant. How is it adapted to living on land? How is it different from the water-dwelling plant?

34

water-dwelling plant in soil | land-dwelling plant in soil | water-dwelling plant in water | land-dwelling plant in water

2 Now, place one water-dwelling plant in a jar of fresh water. Place the land-dwelling plant in the other jar. Plant another land-dwelling plant in one pot and another water-dwelling plant in the other pot. Water the soil in the pots so that it is just damp.

3 Leave all four plants in a sunny area. Every day, observe and record what happens to the plants. Do this for five days. What differences can you observe between the plants?

4 After five days, observe all plants with the magnifying glass. How is each plant suited to its habitat? What happened to the plants placed in habitats other than their normal habitats? Why do you think this happened?

Can Plants Adapt to Different Habitats?

An Explanation

Water-dwelling and land-dwelling plants are well adapted to living in their habitats. Water-dwelling plants, such as *Elodea*, have very thin, small leaves. These plants can get the water they need directly from their habitat. Their stems are usually

FACT: Kelp, a type of giant seaweed, can grow as much as 46 cm (18 in) a day! Kelp likes a saltwater habitat and can form huge forests on the ocean floor.

not very stiff. They float in the water, so their leaves can more easily absorb water. Plants that live on land usually have much thicker leaves to keep water inside. These plants need to get water to their leaves from their roots. Since they live in air, their stems are usually stiffer to hold them upright.

Ideas for Your Science Fair

- How are stream-dwelling plants suited to their habitat?

- How are mosses and lichens suited to their habitats?

- How are saltwater or freshwater plants affected by different water temperatures?

water-dwelling plant
(small, thin leaves and flexible stems)

land-dwelling plants
(broad leaves and stiff stems)

What Happens to Yeast in Cold Water?

How is a living thing, such as yeast, adapted to habitats with different temperatures? Write down your ideas and your reasons for them.

Now Let's Find Out!

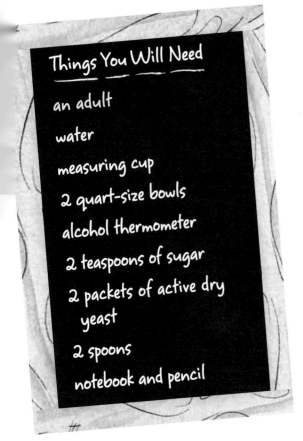

Things You Will Need

an adult

water

measuring cup

2 quart-size bowls

alcohol thermometer

2 teaspoons of sugar

2 packets of active dry yeast

2 spoons

notebook and pencil

1 Put one cup of warm water, no more than 43.5 degrees Celsius (110 degrees Fahrenheit,) in one bowl. Put one cup of ice-cold water in the second bowl. Take the temperature of the water in each bowl. Record this in your notebook.

2 Add one level teaspoon of sugar to each bowl and stir. Sprinkle one package of "active dry" yeast into each

38

bowl and stir again. Yeast is an organism that "sleeps" when it is dry, but "comes to life" when you add it to water.

3 Observe what happens to the living yeast in each bowl. Watch for bubbles coming to the surface. This means the yeast is "blooming." In which bowl does the yeast bloom first? What does this tell you about the best "habitat" for the yeast to grow?

4 Why do you think companies that make yeast for baking put it in very dry packets? What does the yeast need to make it start growing?

What Happens to Yeast in Cold Water?

An Explanation

Active dry yeast is a dormant (sleeping) living thing. It is a fungus that comes alive when you add warm water to it. It also helps to add a bit of sugar as food for the yeast. Once the yeast hits the water, it becomes active and its cells start to divide. It gives off a gas which you can see as bubbles.

FACT: Yeast cells make dough rise when the cells start dividing and give off carbon dioxide gas. The bubbles of carbon dioxide are captured inside the dough and make it bigger.

Yeast blooming

If the water is too cold, it will take a long time for the yeast to grow. If the water is too hot, the yeast will die.

 ## Ideas for Your Science Fair

- Will yeast grow in both freshwater and saltwater?

- Will yeast grow in warm water without sugar?

- Will fresh or active dry yeast grow more quickly in warm water?

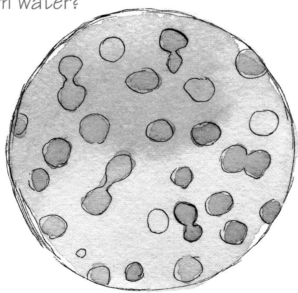

Yeast cells dividing in warm water
(This a drawing of what is seen under a microscope.)

How Do Habitats Regrow in an Empty Area?

In what order do living things re-grow in an empty area? Write down your ideas and your reasons for them.

Now Let's Find Out!

1 You will need to find a safe area close to your home that has been cleared. Fire sometimes clears an area, but it is more likely that you will find an area cleared by people.

Things You Will Need

an adult
area of land that has
    been cleared
camera (optional)
poster board and markers
notebook and pencil

2 Visit the area **with an adult**. Be sure to take your camera, if you can, and your notebook and pencil. Observe the cleared area. Is anything growing there at all? If so, what kinds of plants are there? Record the date and all of your observations in your notebook.

3 Return to the same area every week for at least two months. Each time, record the date and the plant and animal life you observe. Record your data in words, and drawings or photographs (if possible).

4 At the end of the two months, make a poster showing what the area looked like each time you observed it. Did plant life regrow? How did it get there? What happened to the animal life over time? Did animals come back to the area?

How Do Habitats Regrow in an Empty Area?

An Explanation

When an area is cleared, there are usually tiny spores and seeds left behind. Over time, with rain, these will grow into fungi and plants. Fungi usually come back to cleared areas very early. This is because fungi spores are hard to kill and they can survive by living off decaying material. These early living things help to prepare the soil for seeds that are

FACT: Some plants actually need to be in a fire for their seeds to start growing. The seeds of the lodgepole pine tree are covered with sticky resin. When the pine is in a fire, the resin melts and the seeds can be released and grow.

already there or that blow in from other areas. As the plants come back, plant-eating animals return to the area. This whole process is called succession.

 ## Ideas for Your Science Fair

- Does the type of soil in a cleared area affect what grows there first?

- Does the amount of sunlight in a cleared area affect what grows there first?

- What are some ways to keep plants from coming back to a cleared area?

Stages of Succession

cleared ground with fungi spores	fungi, mosses, and lichens	grasses, nonwoody plants, and animals	small trees, shrubs, and animals	tall trees, undergrowth, and animals

45

Words to Know

adaption—A characteristic that suits an organism to its habitat.

carbon dioxide—A gas in the atmosphere that plants use to make food.

cell—The smallest unit of all living things.

decay—To rot.

desert—A type of habitat that stays dry for most of the year.

fungus (fungi, plural)—A simple organism that lives on other organisms.

habitat—A place in which an organism lives.

organism—A living thing.

pigments—The natural colors in organisms.

precipitation—Water from the sky (rain, snow, sleet, or hail).

predators—Animals that hunt other animals for food.

resin—A sticky material made by some plants.

scales—Plates that cover many fish and reptiles.

species—An organism that can breed with others of its own kind.

spores—Parts of fungi that make new fungi.

Learn More

Books

Henderson, Joyce, and Heather Tomasello. *Strategies for Winning Science Fair Projects.* Chichester, England: Wiley, 2001.

Kalman, Bobbie, and John Crossingham. *Land Habitats.* New York: Crabtree Publishing Company, 2007.

Pascoe, Elaine. *Forest Floor.* Farmington Hills, Mich.: Blackbirch Press, 2005.

Stetson, Emily. *Kids' Easy-to-create Wildlife Habitats.* Nashville, Tenn.: Williamson Books, 2004.

Tocci, Salvatore. *Marine Habitats: Life in Salt Water.* New York: Scholastic, Inc., 2004.

Internet Addresses

Amazing Animals.
http://kids.nationalgeographic.com/Animals/

Cool Science.
http://www.hhmi.org/coolscience/index.html

Create a Backyard Habitat.
http://birdwebsite.com/backyard.htm

Index